The Solitude Practice

A Four-Session Guide to Solitude in the Way of Jesus

WaterBrook

John Mark Comer and Practicing the Way

WaterBrook
An imprint of the Penguin Random House Christian Publishing Group,
a division of Penguin Random House LLC
1745 Broadway, New York, NY 10019
waterbrookmultnomah.com
penguinrandomhouse.com

A WaterBrook Trade Paperback Original

Published in association with Yates & Yates, www.yates2.com.

Originally self-published by Practicing the Way (practicingtheway.org) in 2023.

All photos courtesy of Practicing the Way.

Trade Paperback ISBN 978-0-593-60329-1
Ebook ISBN 978-0-593-60330-7

Printed in the United States of America on acid-free paper

1st Printing

Book and cover design by Practicing the Way.

For details on special quantity discounts for bulk purchases, contact
specialmarketscms@penguinrandomhouse.com.

The authorized representative in the EU for product safety and compliance is Penguin Random House Ireland, Morrison Chambers, 32 Nassau Street, Dublin D02 YH68, Ireland. https://eu-contact.penguin.ie

Contents

PART 01

Getting Started

Welcome

The spiritual writer Henri Nouwen once said that "solitude is not a private, therapeutic place. Rather, it is the place of . . . encounter."*

We live in a therapeutic culture, where far more emphasis is put on feeling good than being good. Inside a culture focused on wellness spirituality, it's easy to view practices like solitude, silence, and stillness as no more than spiritual disciplines for introverts who like that sort of thing.

But this is not the solitude of Jesus, or John the Baptist, or Elijah the prophet, or any of the great ones of the Way. For them, solitude wasn't a day spa for the soul. They may have spent time resting in the quiet, but ultimately, the goal wasn't to run away from the world but to run to God. And then come back to the world to love and serve.

You see solitude all over the life of Jesus. As the Gospel writer Luke put it, "Jesus often withdrew to lonely places and prayed."**

And yet: In the digital age, it is now possible to go your entire life without ever being truly alone with God. Our devices keep us tethered to the world of noise and regularly drown out the voice of God in our hearts. We are starved for solitude, living through a global famine of quiet—noise refugees, seeking a new home where we can find rest in God.

Solitude is not an easy path, but it is the ancient path—the Jesus path—to a strong, deep, joyful, vibrant life with God.

Welcome to Practice of solitude.

---

*Henri Nouwen, *The Way of the Heart: Connecting with God Through Prayer, Wisdom, and Silence* (Ballantine, 1983), 14–15.

** Luke 5v16.

The Nine Practices

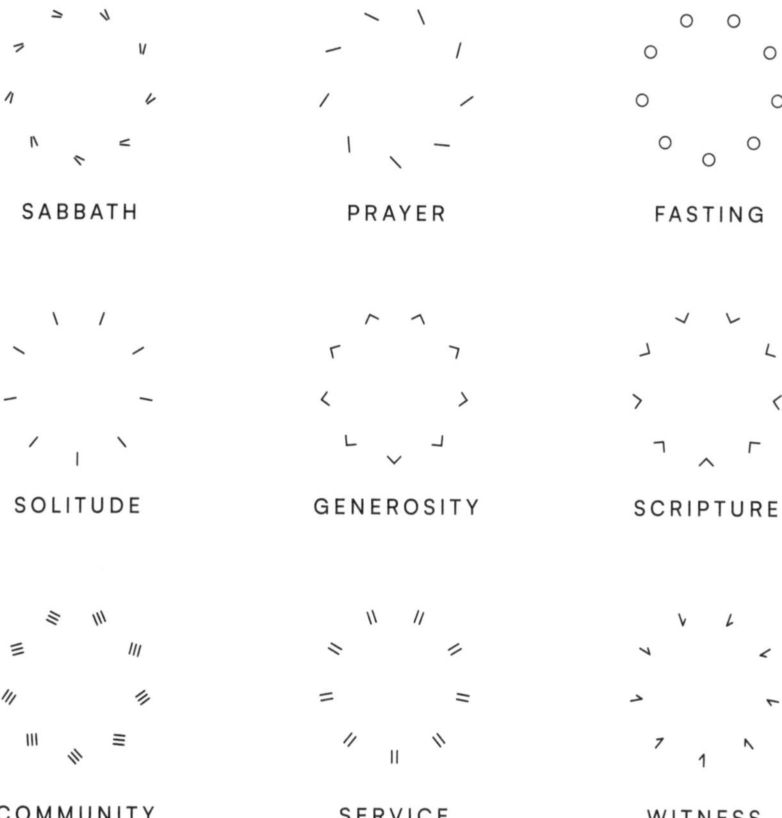

Solitude is just one of nine core Practices in the body of resources available from Practicing the Way. The Practices are spiritual disciplines centered on the life rhythms of Jesus. They are designed not to add even more to your already overbusy life but to slow you down and create space for the Spirit of God to form you to be with Jesus, become like him, and do what he did. Ultimately, they are a way to experience the love of God.

To run another Practice or learn more, turn to page 104.

How to Use This Guide

A few things you need to know

This Practice is designed to be done in community, whether with a few friends around a table, within your small group, in a larger class format, or with your entire church.

The Practice is four sessions long. We recommend meeting together every week or every other week. For those of you who want to spend more time on this Practice, we've included an additional four weeks of bonus conversations in the appendix to go deeper in Scripture and discussion. You are welcome to pause for these conversations in between sessions or skip over them.

You will all need a copy of this Companion Guide. You can purchase a print or ebook version from your preferred retailer or find a free digital PDF at launch.practicingtheway.org. We recommend the print version so you can stay away from your devices during the Practices, as well as take notes during each session. But we realize that digital works better for some.

Each session should take about one to two hours, depending on how long you allow for discussion and whether or not you begin with a meal. See the sample session on the following page.

Are you a group leader or facilitator? Log in to your online Dashboard or sign up at launch.practicingtheway.org to find ideas, best practices, and tips on running this Practice. Page 108 also offers helpful information and tips.

Our Practices are designed to work in a variety of group sizes and environments. For that reason, your gatherings may include additional elements like meals or worship time or may follow a structure slightly different from the following sample. Please adapt as you see fit.

Sample Session

Here is what a typical session could look like.

Welcome

Welcome the group and open in prayer.

Introduction (2–3 min.)

Watch the introduction to the session and pause the video when indicated for your first discussion.

Discussion 01: Practice reflection in triads (15–20 min.)

Process your previous week's spiritual exercise in smaller groups of three to five people with the questions in the Guide.

Teaching (20 min.)

Watch the teaching portion of the video.

Discussion 02: Group conversation (15–30 min.)

Pause the video when indicated for a group-wide conversation.

Testimony and tutorial (5–10 min.)

Watch the rest of the video.

Prayer to close

Close by praying the liturgy in the Guide or however you choose.

The Weekly Rhythm

The four sessions of this Practice are designed to follow a four-part rhythm that is based on our model of spiritual formation.

01 Learn

Gather together as a community for an interactive experience of learning about the Way of Jesus through teaching, storytelling, and discussion. Bring your Guide to the session and follow along.

02 Practice

On your own, before the next session, go and "put it into practice," as Jesus himself said.* We will provide weekly spiritual exercises to integrate this practice into your everyday life, as well as recommended resources to go deeper.

03 Reflect

Reflection is key to spiritual formation. After your practice and before the next session, set aside 10–15 minutes to reflect on your experience. Reflection questions are included in this Guide at the end of each session.

04 Process together

When you come back together, watch the introduction, and then start by sharing your reflections with your group. This moment is crucial because we need one another to process our lives before God and make sense of our stories. If you are meeting in a larger group, you will need to break into smaller subgroups for this conversation so everyone has a chance to share.

* Philippians 4v9.

Tips on Beginning a New Practice

This Guide is full of spiritual exercises, time-tested strategies, and good advice on the spiritual discipline of solitude.

But it's important to note that the Practices are not formulaic. We can't use them to control our spiritual formation or even our relationship with God. Sometimes they don't even work very well. Sometimes we go into solitude and experience God's presence like never before, but other times we just feel bored and distracted. That's normal.

The key with the spiritual disciplines is to let go of outcomes and just offer them up to Jesus in love.

Because it's so easy to lose sight of the ultimate aim of a Practice, here are a few tips to keep in mind as you enter into solitude.

01 Start small

Start where you are, not where you "should" be. It's counterintuitive, but the smaller the start, the better chance you have of really sticking to it and growing over time.

02 Think subtraction, not addition

Don't try to "add" solitude into your already overbusy, overfull life. You are likely already stressed and tired. Instead, think, *What can I cut out of my daily schedule? How can I slow my life down? Where can I find a little breathing room to rest and pray?*

Formation is about less, not more. About slowing down and simplifying your life around what matters most: life with Jesus.

03 You get out what you put in

The more fully you give yourself to this Practice, the more life-changing it will be; the more you just dabble with it, the more shortcuts you take, the less of an effect it will have on your transformation.

04 Remember the J curve

Experts on learning tell us that mastering a new skill tends to follow a J-shaped curve; we tend to get worse before we get better. You may enjoy a quiet morning before work or a lazy Sunday afternoon, but when you go into solitude, you may feel itchy or anxious or emotional. That's okay. Expect it to be a bit awkward at first; it will get easier in time. Just stay with the Practice.

05 There is no formation without repetition

Spiritual formation is slow, deep, cumulative work that happens over years, not weeks. The goal of this four-week experience is just to get you started on a journey of a lifetime. Upon completion of this Practice, you will have a map for the journey ahead and hopefully some possible companions for the Way.

But what you do next is up to you.

Before You Begin

The following resources are designed to enhance your experience of the Solitude Practice, but they are entirely optional.

Recommended reading

Reading a book alongside the Practice can greatly enhance your understanding and enjoyment of this discipline. You may love to read, or you may not. For that reason, it's recommended but certainly not required.

The recommended reading for the Solitude Practice is *Invitation to Solitude and Silence* by Ruth Haley Barton.

Ruth Haley Barton is a spiritual guide and author well known for her deep insights into spiritual formation, inner renewal, and contemplative life.

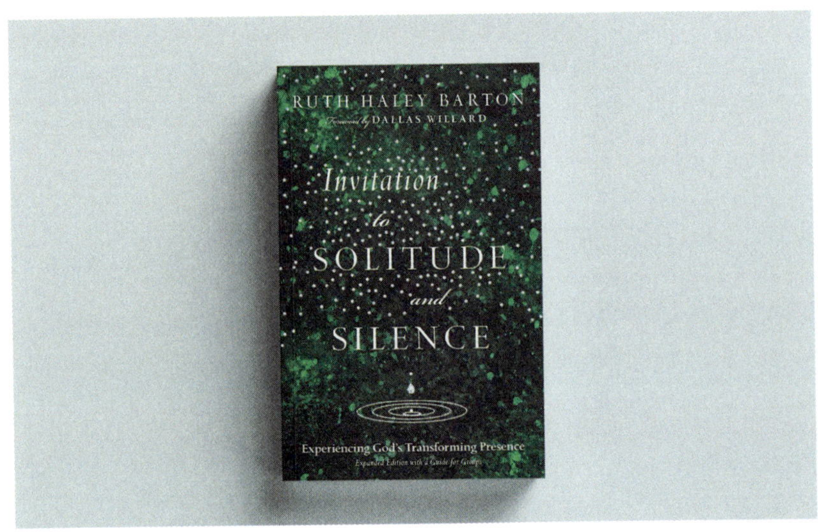

The Spiritual Health Reflection

One final note: Before you begin Session 01, please set aside 20–30 minutes and take the Spiritual Health Reflection. This is a self-assessment we developed in partnership with pastors and leading experts in spiritual formation. It's designed to help you reflect on the health of your soul in order to better name Jesus' invitations to you as you follow the Way.

You can come back to the Spiritual Health Reflection as often as you'd like (we recommend one to two times a year) to chart your growth and continue to move forward on your spiritual journey.

To access the Spiritual Health Reflection, visit practicingtheway.org/reflection and create an account. Answer the prompt questions slowly and prayerfully.

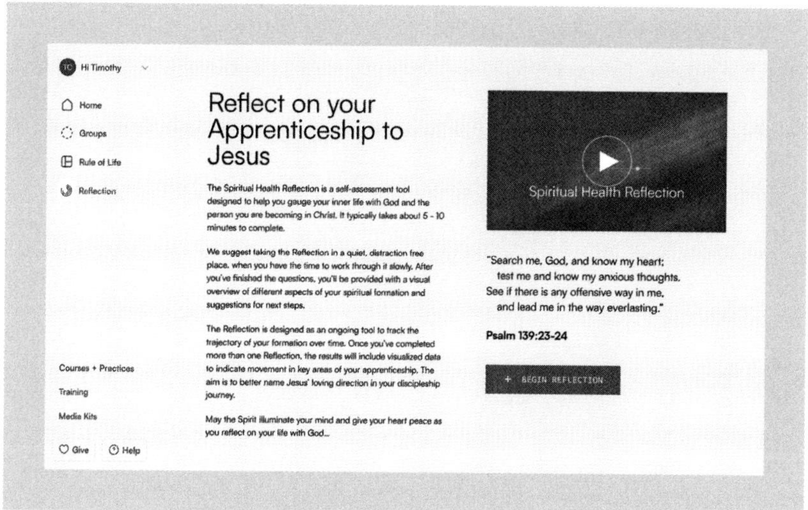

The Practicing the Way Primer

If this is your first time engaging with a Practicing the Way resource, we invite you to set aside 15 minutes before Session 01 to watch a primer on spiritual formation. This will give you a brief overview of the *why* behind spiritual practices and key insights to guard and guide your coming practice.

Log in to your online Dashboard, or sign up to watch the primer at launch.practicingtheway.org.

PART 02

The Sessions

SESSION 01

The Quiet Place

Overview

The world is getting louder and louder with each passing year.

Smartphones, alerts, Wi-Fi, email, social media, streaming services, and the endless queue of entertainment—the noise of the digital age is with us 24/7.

This poses a major problem for those of us who apprentice under Jesus. All the saints and sages have said for millennia that the two primary places we discover God are in community—deep, long-term, loving relationships with other apprentices of Jesus in the family of God—and in solitude, silence, and stillness.

You see this pattern in the life of Jesus himself, where he would regularly retreat to slip away into the *eremos*, or "the deserted place," for solitude with his Father, to draw on the Holy Spirit for strength, wisdom, direction, and joy. Then he would come back into the world of people to love and serve.

This back-and-forth rhythm of community and solitude is one we desperately need to reclaim for the modern age. Most of us get intuitively that we need relationships with other followers of Jesus to flourish, but many of us are less in touch with our need for intentional times in the quiet—to be alone with ourselves and our God. How do we befriend God, and let God befriend us, amid all the noise, distraction, and busyness of modern life?

We follow Jesus' example: We go into solitude.

Opening Questions

When instructed, circle up in triads (smaller groups of three to five people) and discuss the following questions:

01 Is solitude a practice in your life right now?

02 How are you hoping to grow in solitude over the next few weeks?

03 What support do you need from this community as we go on this journey with God?

Teaching

Key Scripture

Luke 5v15–16

Session summary

- The Greek word *eremos* or "the deserted place" can also be translated as the solitary or quiet place.
- Jesus' life had a rhythm of retreating for solitude and returning for service.
- Solitude is not:
    - **Loneliness —** it's not inner emptiness but inner fulfillment.
    - **Isolation —** it's not moving away from but toward relationship with God.
    - **Aloneness —** it's not a preference-based time away from others.
- Solitude is intentional time in the quiet with ourselves and God.
- The practice of solitude has two companions: silence and stillness.

Teaching Notes

As you watch Session 01 together, feel free to use these pages to take notes.

Discussion Questions

Now it's time for a conversation about the teaching. Pause the video for a few minutes to discuss these questions in small groups:

01 What stuck out to you from that teaching? Was there a Scripture or thought that especially resonated with you?

02 What are some examples of internal noise in your life? What are some examples of external noise in your life?

03 What do you hope the practice of solitude will add to your life? How could a rhythm of solitude help you connect to the voice and presence of God?

Practice Notes

As you continue to watch Session 01 together, feel free to use this page to take notes.

Closing Prayer

Take a few deep breaths, become aware of God's presence, and pray this prayer slowly, leaving short silence between each line.

God the Father,
Jesus the Son,
Holy Spirit,
we long to encounter you.
Grant us courage to follow you
out from the noise, into the solitary place,
knowing that whatever awaits us there,
you, too, will be found.

Amen.

Exercise

Begin your day with a few minutes of solitude, silence, and stillness.

You may find this exercise works better for you at night before bed, midmorning while your toddler is napping, or on your lunch break; that's great. But for the vast majority of people, we recommend first thing in the morning, when your body is rested, your heart is open, and the day is new.

Here's a step-by-step exercise to try:

01 Find a quiet place in your home or outside in nature that is as distraction-free as possible. Make sure your phone is in another room, and settle into a comfortable position.

02 Begin to take long, slow breaths from your belly all the way up through your lungs. Inhale through your nose; exhale through your mouth. If you want, count up five seconds on the inhale and down five seconds on the exhale.

03 With each inhale, prayerfully welcome the Father, the Son, and the Holy Spirit into the deepest place within you. You may want to repeat a simple prayer like "Come, Holy Spirit" or "Lord, have mercy on me" or just "Jesus." Something to keep your mind focused and to let this be more than just breathing, but prayer.

- Your mind will seize this opportunity to run wild with thoughts, feelings, memories, to-dos, and distractions. That's okay. Don't judge yourself, feel bad, give up, or worry. Distraction doesn't mean you're "bad" at prayer; it means you're human. When you notice your mind starting to wander, just come back to your breathing or your prayer word.

- In the beginning, just one to two minutes of this type of prayer is a win. Ten minutes is a home run.

04 Now that you are centered in your body and in God, spend a few minutes just resting in God's love for you. Let the Holy Spirit make his presence known to your whole body. Just soak in his love, peace, and joy. Let God love you.

- You may want to visualize the love of the Father being poured out in Christ and into the depth of your being by the Holy Spirit.
- Or you may want to listen for God's voice and see what comes to mind.
- Or you may want to worship and express your love to God in your own way.
- But don't try to fill up this time. And don't try to make anything happen or control the experience—just be with God.

05 After a few minutes, you may want to continue your time in solitude by praying a psalm or reading a story from the Gospels or a passage from Scripture. Or by praying over your life. Or by journaling to God. Follow your heart.

06 Whenever you're done, close your time with a simple prayer of gratitude to God for his presence, love, and goodness in your life.

Please note: Our strong recommendation is that you do this every single day this coming week and, if you can, for a little longer on the Sabbath. If you get to do it only once or twice, that's still great, but there is something about the practice of beginning every day in the quiet with God that is very basic, yet ancient and powerful.

This practice of beginning your day in silent prayer is not for everybody; it may not work best for your personality or stage of life. But so many of the great followers of Jesus throughout history tell us that the way to begin to be with Jesus all the time is to set aside our first moments upon waking to intentionally be with him for some of the time.

Reach Exercise

Practice solitude for a full hour each morning before you touch your phone.

Afterward spend your remaining time as you feel moved—reading Scripture, listening for God's voice, offering petition and intercession, journaling, or whatever you feel a stirring in your heart toward. Follow your desire for God wherever it leads.

We all learn differently. Some of us prefer reading, others listening, and others doing. If you'd like to go deeper, choose what resonates with you and give it a try.

A Special Note on Retreats

With spiritual exercises, it's always best to start very small and slowly work your way up. Don't try to be heroic; be gentle with yourself, as God is gentle. That said, for the final session of our Solitude Practice, we're going to invite you to go on retreat. A daily quiet time is an essential practice, but there are some things that can happen only in longer periods of solitude.

You may choose to begin with just a few hours of retreat, or you may want to go away for a half day or full day. Or you may choose to go away overnight or even for a few days. If so, you will need to begin planning now.

Look for retreat centers near you, or monasteries—they usually have guest rooms available for people who want to go pray in the quiet. You may have access to a family cabin or empty guesthouse, or you may choose to rent a cabin or quiet place to be alone. And if you don't have access to a place to go on retreat, just follow Jesus' example and go outside. Go on a long hike or camping by yourself, or just find a place in nature to be alone.

Those of you with children may want to alternate days away with your spouse or call on your community and/or family for help at home. This practice of retreat can be a time for your community to come together. One of the best gifts we can give one another is the gift of time away to rest and be with God. Communities can share the gift of solitude and Sabbath with those members who don't have easy access to it.

Practice Reflection

Reflection is a key component in our spiritual formation.

Millennia ago, King David prayed in Psalm 139v23–24:

> Search me, God, and know my heart;
>   test me and know my anxious thoughts.
> See if there is any offensive way in me,
>   and lead me in the way everlasting.

South African professor Trevor Hudson has quoted one of his pastoral supervisors as saying, "We do not learn from experience; we learn from reflection upon experience."*

If you want to get the most out of this Practice, you need to do it and then reflect on it.

---

* Trevor Hudson, *A Mile in My Shoes: Cultivating Compassion* (Upper Room Books, 2005), 57.

Before your next time together with the group for Session 02, take 10–15 minutes to journal your answers to the following three questions:

01 How did your practice of solitude go this week?

02 Where did you experience resistance in solitude?

03 In what ways did you encounter God in solitude?

Note: As you write, be as specific as possible. While bullet points are just fine, if you write your insights out in narrative form, your brain will be able to process them in a more lasting way.

Reflection Notes

Keep Growing (Optional)

The following resources were created to enhance your experience of this Practice, but they are entirely optional.

Read

Invitation to Solitude and Silence by Ruth Haley Barton (Chapters 01–03)

Listen

Rule of Life podcast on solitude (Episode 01)

Bonus Conversation

If you would like to slow down this four-week Practice to give your community more time to sit in each week's teaching and spiritual exercise, you can pause and meet for an optional conversation outlined in the appendix.

SESSION 02

Encounter with Our Self

Overview

We often go into solitude tired and worn down by the stress and strain of life in the modern world, and we expect our time in solitude to be like a kind of day spa for the soul. And sometimes it is. But just as often, solitude can feel less like pampering and more like emotional surgery—harrowing, intense, and painful. Because we can get away from others, but we can't escape ourselves.

Often, what we carry into solitude is our pain. We quickly come to realize all that we've been distracting ourselves from, as feelings of exhaustion, worry, sadness, anger, and shame all come up.

Yet, from Jesus, we learn that to be free of our pain, we have to face our pain. On the evening before his crucifixion, in the Garden of Gethsemane, we see Jesus go to the place of pain and meet God there. He gives God his feelings, his desires, and his trust.

It is through this simple but difficult practice of noticing and naming our emotions before God in solitude and prayer, and offering them up to him in raw honesty, that we are deeply formed into the people God has always desired us to become.

Reflection Questions

When instructed, circle up in triads (smaller groups of three to five people) and discuss the following questions:

01 How did your practice of solitude go this week?

02 Where did you experience external or internal resistance in solitude?

03 In what ways did you encounter God in solitude?

Teaching

Key Scripture

Matthew 26v36–39

Session summary

- While we are used to learning by addition—books, teachings, podcasts—the desert teaches by subtraction.
- Often the first movement in solitude is that we encounter pain as our exhaustion, fear, sadness, anger, and shame come to the surface.
- In order to get free of this pain, we have to face it.
- Jesus models how we are to face our pain. We give God:
    - **Our feelings —** we pray whatever is in us.
    - **Our desires —** we honestly offer God the good or the bad that we want.
    - **Our trust —** we give up the illusion of control and surrender.
- We heal when we move beyond our "managed life" to face our "wounded life" below the surface.

Teaching Notes

As you watch Session 02 together, feel free to use these pages to take notes.

Discussion Questions

Now it's time for a conversation about the teaching. Pause the video for a few minutes to discuss these questions in small groups:

01 Have you ever encountered God in a specific area or moment of pain? What was that experience like?

02 What are the most common ways you distract yourself (or allow yourself to be distracted) from the pain in your life?

03 Jesus shows us how to give God our feelings, our desires, and our trust. Which of those do you have the hardest time giving to God? What's one step you could take to surrender that to him?

Practice Notes

As you continue to watch Session 02 together, feel free to use this page to take notes.

Closing Prayer

End your time together by praying this liturgy:

Jesus Christ,
we confess that we have carried
our pain and wounds
to places other than your healing hands.
We now entrust ourselves wholly to you
and say *yes* to facing the pain—known and
unknown to us—confident that
you face it with us.

Amen.

Exercise

Begin your day with a few minutes of solitude, noticing and naming your emotions with Jesus' Gethsemane prayer.

Unlike last session, this time we're also calling you to an exercise of noticing and naming your emotions and then praying Jesus' Gethsemane prayer.

Again, we recommend you do this first thing in the morning, but you may find it works better for you after work, late at night, or at a pause in your day. Just find a time when you are at peace and attentive, and attempt to stick with the same time each day.

Here's a step-by-step exercise to try:

01 Find a quiet place in your home or outside in nature that is as distraction-free as possible. Make sure your phone is in another room, and settle into a comfortable position.

02 Begin to take long, slow breaths from your belly all the way up through your lungs. Inhale through your nose; exhale through your mouth. If you want, count up five seconds on the inhale and down five seconds on the exhale.

03 With each inhale, prayerfully welcome the Father, the Son, and the Holy Spirit into the deepest place within you. You may want to repeat a simple prayer like "Come, Holy Spirit," "Lord, have mercy on me," or just "Jesus." This helps keep your mind focused and turns breathing into prayer.

- Your mind will seize this opportunity to run wild with thoughts, feelings, memories, to-dos, and distractions. That's okay. Don't judge yourself, feel bad, give up, or worry. Distraction doesn't mean you're "bad" at prayer; it means you're human. When you notice your mind starting to wander, just return to your breathing or prayer word.
- In the beginning, just one or two minutes of this type of prayer is a win. Ten minutes is a home run.

04 Now that you are centered in your body and in God, let yourself feel whatever is in you. Don't fight it, run from it, feel guilty about it, or judge it—just notice it. Let the feeling be. Then name the emotion as specifically as possible. You may want to use the following list of emotions. Pick out one to three feeling words that describe your experience.

Happy	Sad	Angry	Scared	Confused
Admired	Alienated	Abused	Afraid	Ambivalent
Alive	Ashamed	Aggravated	Alarmed	Awkward
Appreciated	Burdened	Agitated	Anxious	Baffled
Assured	Condemned	Anguished	Appalled	Bewildered
Cheerful	Crushed	Annoyed	Apprehensive	Bothered
Confident	Defeated	Betrayed	Awed	Constricted
Content	Dejected	Cheated	Concerned	Directionless
Delighted	Demoralized	Coerced	Defensive	Disorganized
Determined	Depressed	Controlled	Desperate	Distracted
Ecstatic	Deserted	Deceived	Doubtful	Doubtful
Elated	Despised	Disgusted	Fearful	Flustered
Encouraged	Devastated	Dismayed	Frantic	Foggy
Energized	Disappointed	Displeased	Full of Dread	Hesitant
Enthusiastic	Discarded	Dominated	Guarded	Immobilized
Excited	Discouraged	Enraged	Horrified	Misunderstood
Exuberant	Disgraced	Exasperated	Impatient	Perplexed

05 Just sit in those feelings. Sink into them. Normally, we turn away from them and run in the opposite direction. Instead, turn and face them. Like you would an ocean wave, let it wash over you and then pass you by.

06 Then, pray Jesus' Gethsemane prayer.

- Give God your feelings: Tell him what you are feeling, with no filter.
- Give God your desires: Tell him what you really want, good or bad.
- Give God your trust: Surrender your heart again to him. Stop grasping for control, and yield yourself to God and his will for your life. You may want to pray Jesus' own prayer, "Not my will, but yours be done."

07 Whenever you're done, close your time with a simple prayer of gratitude to God for his presence, love, and goodness in your life.

Please note: Our strong recommendation is that you do this every single day this coming week, but the exercise of noticing and naming your emotions may take a bit longer. You may want to save that for a point in your week where you have unhurried time to sit with God in prayer, like your Sabbath or day off.

Reach Exercise

Go for a solitude walk in creation.

Most of Jesus' solitude time was spent outdoors in the beauty of his Father's world. He was in the quiet but also surrounded by the gentle sound of birds and animals and wind and rivers and rocks and trees. Try doing a solitary walk this week, ideally somewhere beautiful if you have access to a state park or hiking trail. If not, just find a park near your house and be with God in creation. Try to really notice the beauty all around you. Receive it as a gift from God. As you walk, let yourself feel whatever comes up and let God work deep within you as you offer your time to him.

A Special Note on Retreats

Just a reminder that our final session's exercise is to go on retreat. We recommend you schedule a time and place now so you can experience this special gift of an extended time in solitude.

Practice Reflection

Before your next time together with the group for Session 03, take 10–15 minutes to journal your answers to the following three questions:

01 How did your practice of solitude go this session?

02 Where did you experience resistance in solitude, whether external or internal?

03 In what ways did you encounter God in solitude?

Note: As you write, be as specific as possible. While bullet points are just fine, if you write your insights out in narrative form, your brain will be able to process them in a more lasting way.

Reflection Notes

Keep Growing (Optional)

The following resources were created to enhance your experience of this Practice, but they are entirely optional.

Read

Invitation to Solitude and Silence by Ruth Haley Barton (Chapters 04–06)

Listen

Rule of Life podcast on solitude (Episode 02)

Bonus Conversation

If you would like to slow down this four-week Practice to give your community more time to sit in each week's teaching and spiritual exercise, you can pause and meet for an optional conversation outlined in the appendix.

SESSION 03

Encounter with Our Enemy

Overview

In the fourth century A.D., when the Way of Jesus was legalized in the Roman Empire and the community of Jesus morphed from a persecuted minority to a political majority, thousands of serious disciples—now referred to as the desert fathers and mothers—left the corruption and compromise of the church behind. Rather than pursue a "normal life" in an absurd world, they fled into the quiet of the desert to seek God in solitude.

One of their major insights on solitude was that it was not Sabbath rest but spiritual war. They pointed out that Jesus went out into the *eremos* to fight, not to flee; to engage, not to escape; to win victory, not to give up.

They also developed a theological construct they called "the three enemies of the soul"—the world, the flesh, and the devil—seeing discipleship as a kind of spiritual war against this unholy trinity.

In the desert, not only do we encounter ourselves and all our feelings, but we also engage in a battle with these enemies—the world, which is a vast conspiracy against quiet and solitude; our own flesh, which comes up with all sorts of emotionally loaded reasons not to go away; and the devil himself, who is always there to draw us away from Jesus' call to the *eremos*.

But if we are willing to fight the resistance and go into solitude, it may be hard at first, yet long-term, it yields dividends of freedom.

Reflection Questions

When instructed, circle up in triads (smaller groups of three to five people) and discuss the following questions:

01 How did your practice of solitude go this week?

02 Where did you experience resistance in solitude?

03 In what ways did you encounter God in solitude?

Teaching

Key Scripture

Matthew 4v1–11

Session summary

- When we go into solitude, we encounter the three enemies of the soul:
    - **The world** — the system of ideas, values, practices, and social norms of a sinful society
    - **The flesh** — our base drives for self-gratification
    - **The devil** — the spiritual being animating the force of evil in our souls and society
- We can expect to experience resistance—through mysterious human and nonhuman forces—around the practice of solitude.
- The freedom that ultimately comes from solitude is won by persevering in the struggle against these resistances.

Teaching Notes

As you watch Session 03 together, feel free to use these pages to take notes.

Discussion Questions

Now it's time for a conversation about the teaching. Pause the video for a few minutes to discuss these questions in small groups:

01 A lot of us might fear the desert because it's challenging. What resistance might you need to work through as you enter the desert place of solitude?

02 Have you ever thought about the desert as a place of strength? Where can you see this play out in your own life?

03 How might remembering that solitude is a place of resisting the world, the flesh, and the devil help you in your practice of solitude?

Practice Notes

As you continue to watch Session 03 together, feel free to use this page to take notes.

Closing Prayer

End your time together by praying this liturgy:

Holy Spirit, we heed your invitation
to enter the wilderness—not to
flee from our adversaries, but to
contend by your power with them there.
Jesus Christ, you who are far above
all powers and authorities,
free us here that we may also share
in the freedom of those around us.

Amen.

Exercise

Engage in *Lectio Divina.*

In the previous two sessions, we've been starting each day with a few minutes in silence before we touch our phones or rush out the door. We encourage you to continue this practice of beginning your day in quiet prayer—not only for the next two sessions, but for the rest of your life.

But this session, we want to invite you to go further in your practice of solitude. The goal of being alone with God in silence is, ultimately, to hear God's voice over all the other voices in our heads—especially from the three enemies of our souls. And the ultimate litmus test of the truth of God over the lies of these enemies is found in Scripture. That's why, in solitude, when Jesus was confronted with lies from the enemy, he calmly quoted Scripture to anchor himself in God's truth.

This week's exercise is called *Lectio Divina*, which is a Latin phrase meaning "spiritual reading." It's an ancient way of reading Scripture slowly and prayerfully, listening for God's voice over your life.

Lectio Divina has four simple movements:

01 Read a passage from Scripture very slowly and prayerfully, and pay special attention to any words, phrases, or thoughts that seem to stand out to you or touch you emotionally in any way. Look for what "shimmers." You can pick any passage of Scripture, but we recommend you start with a psalm or a selection from the Gospels or a New Testament letter.

02 Reflect. Reread the passage, this time lingering over the words or phrases that feel highlighted to you. Just turn them over slowly in your mind, thinking about what God may be saying to you.

03 Respond by praying those impressions back to God.

04 Rest in God's loving word to you. Let your whole body slow down and sink into God's presence and peace.

We recommend you practice *Lectio Divina* several times this coming week. As you think about this coming week, consider when you would like to engage in this practice. You can do this each morning after your breath prayer, on your Sabbath, or anytime you like. Also, take time beforehand to determine the passage(s) you want to read through in these set-aside times, or take some recommendations for these from your community.

Reach Exercise

Establish a digital Sabbath.

One reason solitude is more important now than it's ever been is that we are the first generation to apprentice under Jesus in the digital age. We are still learning how to pray and have a rich inner life with God inside a wider culture of distraction, noise, hurry, and superficiality.

Many people have found that one of the most helpful disciplines for our era is a digital Sabbath—one full day a week when all your devices, including your smartphone, are either powered fully off or drastically limited. Even doctors are beginning to recommend this practice, simply for the health of your central nervous system. How much more so for those who desire to experience God's nearness in our everyday lives?

If a full day is too much for you, you may want to start with a half day or even a few hours on your Sabbath or Sunday afternoon. And if you need to be available by phone, you might consider getting a landline for your home or turning off all alerts and only briefly checking your phone at set times during the day.

If you're interested in learning more about the Practice of Sabbath, you can find resources at practicingtheway.org/sabbath.

Practice Reflection

Before your next time together with the group for Session 04, take 10–15 minutes to journal your answers to the following three questions:

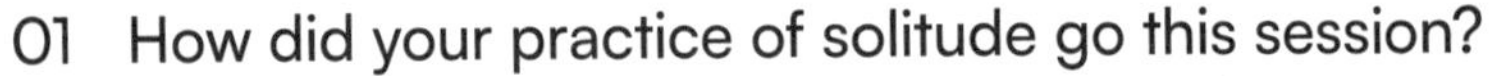

01 How did your practice of solitude go this session?

02 Where did you experience resistance in solitude?

03 In what ways did you encounter God in solitude?

Note: As you write, be as specific as possible. While bullet points are just fine, if you write out your insights in narrative form, your brain will be able to process them in a more lasting way.

Reflection Notes

Keep Growing (Optional)

The following resources were created to enhance your experience of this Practice, but they are entirely optional.

Read

Invitation to Solitude and Silence by Ruth Haley Barton (Chapters 07–09)

Listen

Rule of Life podcast on solitude (Episode 03)

Bonus Conversation

If you would like to slow down this four-week Practice to give your community more time to sit in each week's teaching and spiritual exercise, you can pause and meet for an optional conversation outlined in the appendix.

SESSION 04

Encounter with Our God

Overview

Solitude is the place of encounter.

We go into "the desert" to encounter our selves and all the emotions that live below the surface of our lives. And we go to encounter our enemy and get free of our hearts' entanglements with the world, the flesh, and the devil. But ultimately, we go into the quiet to encounter God.

We go into solitude because we ache for God in the deepest places of our beings. We go because there is nothing like God's presence. We go to listen for his voice, to hear him speak over each of us our identity and calling.

This is why most of our time in solitude is just spent quietly listening. In a world of noise and distraction, it comes as no surprise that quiet is the primary medium in which we hear God's voice to us. This back-and-forth of speaking and listening to God is the heart not only of communication, but of communion with God.

As important as it is to receive our identities and callings as gifts from God's hand, ultimately, the most important thing that happens in solitude is that we love and are loved by God.

Reflection Questions

When instructed, circle up in triads (smaller groups of three to five people) and discuss the following questions:

01 How did your practice of solitude go this week?

02 Where did you experience resistance in solitude?

03 In what ways did you encounter God in solitude?

Teaching

Key Scripture

Mark 1v32–39

Session summary

- Solitude is not a private therapeutic place, but the place of encounter with:
    - Our self,
    - our enemy,
    - and, finally, our God.
- When we encounter God in solitude, we can each emerge with a clearer vision of:
    - Our identity — who we are in God.
    - Our calling — what we are to do next with God.
- We need to learn to listen for God's voice through Scripture, life circumstances, whispers to our hearts, and our mind's thoughts.
- We can practice solitude in an ongoing way by incorporating it into our Rules of Life and actively "de-noising" our lives.

Teaching Notes

As you watch Session 04 together, feel free to use these pages to take notes.

Discussion Questions

Now it's time for a conversation about the teaching. Pause the video for a few minutes to discuss these questions in small groups:

01 Whether big or small, have you ever had an encounter with God in solitude? What was that experience like?

02 In light of your experience with solitude throughout this course, what is God doing in you during your "retreating" that you want to carry into your "returning"?

03 How do you want to integrate solitude into your life going forward?

Practice Notes

As you continue to watch Session 04 together, feel free to use this page to take notes.

Closing Prayer

End your time together by praying this liturgy:

Jesus Christ, our Good Shepherd,
you have not withheld
your voice from our lives.
Amid the noise of all other voices,
may we recognize yours—within us and
around us—and be found as those
who listen and obey.

Amen.

Exercise

Engage in listening prayer.

Our final exercise for this Practice is listening prayer. We encourage you to continue beginning your day in the quiet before you turn to your phone. We recommend you add this exercise to your new morning rhythm, but you may choose another time.

Whenever you choose, this exercise is built on the theological truth that our bodies are "temples of the Holy Spirit"*; the Spirit of God has direct access to your mind and imagination. He can interject his thoughts into your thoughts and his desires into your desires. Learning to make space for this to happen, and to discern his voice from all the other voices in our heads, is a key task of discipleship to Jesus.

The exercise itself is very simple:

01 Find a quiet, distraction-free time and place, put away your phone, and get comfortable.

02 Take a few minutes to just breathe deeply, in and out. You may want to simply say "Father" or "Come, Holy Spirit" as you inhale each breath. Let yourself slow down.

03 When you're ready to begin, ask God to silence the voice of the enemy, to clear out of your mind and the air around you any voices that are not the voice of God.

04 Then, ask God to speak to you. This can be as simple as praying, "God, please speak to me," or "God, is there anything you want to say to me?"

* 1 Corinthians 6v19.

05 Finally, open your mind and heart to God's Spirit and listen. What comes to mind may be any of these:

- A line or passage of Scripture
- A word or phrase
- A thought or feeling
- A picture in your mind
- A sequence of pictures that "play" like a short film in your imagination
- A memory
- Something you have recently thought about, read, heard, or seen

Don't feel like you have to strain. Just wait quietly. Often, the very first thought that comes to mind is from God. Something may come, or it may not—either way is fine. Our job is just to listen, not to make God speak.

06 Discern. It's very important that you test everything you "hear" against Scripture and in community. Don't be afraid to check it against the Bible, talk to your pastor, or share it with other followers of Jesus. This is the practice of discernment, and it's something we do together.

07 Reflect and rest. If something comes to mind, spend a little time reflecting on it, asking the Spirit to clarify in your mind the meaning of his word to you. Write it down so you can remember it and spend more time in reflection in the coming days.

Consider in this coming week when you would like to engage in this practice. Our recommendation is that you do this exercise daily, but you might just want to practice it once or twice this week. The goal is to begin really listening deeply for God's voice in your life and learning to live off his words to you.

Reach Exercise

Go on a solitude retreat.

For our final reach exercise, we invite you to go away, slow down, and enter into this experience of God through the practice of retreat.

We've been dipping our toes in the water of solitude for the last three sessions; now it's time to dive all the way in. Ten minutes of silence is a great way to begin your day, but some things can happen only in longer periods of solitude. The spiritual life has its own pace, and it's slow, not hurried.

Any quiet place will do—a retreat center, monastery, cabin, guesthouse, campground, park, or even your own home if no one is around and all your devices are powered off. Find your "desert."

There's no "right" length of time to go away. You may choose to go overnight or even for a few days. Many cities have monasteries within driving distance, and they usually offer silent retreats for anyone interested. Or you may just want to go away for a few hours.

There's no "right" way to spend your time on retreat. In fact, be careful not to overfill it with spiritual busyness.

Here's what a day on retreat could look like:

8–9 a.m.: Prepare your mind and heart to hear from God. Take a walk, spend time breathing, or do whatever will help you set aside the worry and distraction of your current life. Try to arrange your morning so you can remain in silence from the time you wake up until after your retreat.

9–11 a.m.: Read and meditate on Scripture through *Lectio Divina*, taking time to stop and reflect when God seems to be speaking to you through the text. Spend time in listening prayer.

11 a.m.–12 p.m.: Journal or write down your heart's response to what you have read or heard. Pray your heart back to God.

12–1 p.m.: Eat lunch and take a walk, reflecting on the morning.

1–2 p.m.: Take a nap or rest.

2–3 p.m.: Clarify any direction you sense from the Spirit of God over the coming season of your life.

3–4 p.m.: Write down any direction and other thoughts in a journal. Thank God for your time together, and ask whether there is anything else he wants to say. Prayerfully prepare to reenter the flow of life.

Again, this is just one possible schedule. There's no "right" way to be with God on retreat. The key is to make space for rest, quiet, listening, reflection, and prayer.

You may feel close to God, or you may not. You may "hear" a word from God, or you may not. You might feel happy, sad, anxious, or weary. That's okay. Just let the experience be what it is and offer it to God for your healing and in loving trust.

The more you practice retreat, the more you will come to relax into it, enjoy it, and look forward to it. But this may take time. Just stay with it and wait for God in the quiet.

Practice Reflection

As you come to the end of this Practice, take 10–15 minutes to journal your answers to the following three questions:

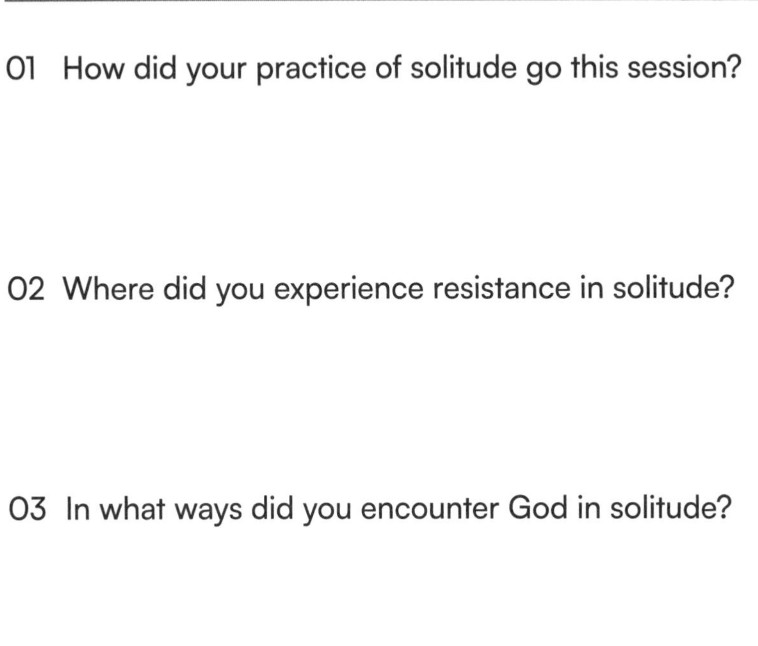

01 How did your practice of solitude go this session?

02 Where did you experience resistance in solitude?

03 In what ways did you encounter God in solitude?

Note: As you write, be as specific as possible. While bullet points are just fine, if you write out your insights in narrative form, your brain will be able to process them in a more lasting way.

Reflection Notes

Keep Growing (Optional)

The following resources were created to enhance your experience of this Practice, but they are entirely optional.

Read

Invitation to Solitude and Silence by Ruth Haley Barton (Chapters 10–12)

Listen

Rule of Life podcast on solitude (Episode 04)

Bonus Conversation

If you would like to slow down this four-week Practice to give your community more time to sit in each week's teaching and spiritual exercise, you can pause and meet for an optional conversation outlined in the appendix.

May the peace
of Christ be
with you.

PART 03

Continue the Journey

Recommended Reading

Here are some of our favorite books on the Practice of solitude for those of you who desire to learn more:

Invitation to Solitude and Silence

by Ruth Haley Barton

The Power of Silence

by Robert Cardinal Sarah

The Way of the Heart

by Henri Nouwen

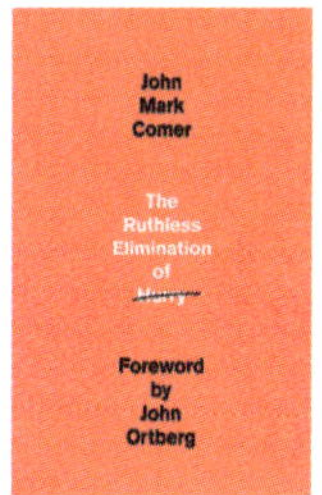

The Ruthless Elimination of Hurry

by John Mark Comer

Poustinia: Encountering God in Silence, Solitude, and Prayer

by Catherine Doherty

The Practices

Information alone isn't enough to produce transformation.

By adopting not just the teaching but also the practices from Jesus' own life, we open up our entire beings to God and allow him to transform us into people of love.

Our nine core Practices work together to form a Rule of Life for the modern era.

Sabbath	**Prayer**	**Fasting**
Solitude	**Generosity**	**Scripture**
Community	**Service**	**Witness**

WHAT'S INCLUDED FOR EACH PRACTICE

Four Sessions

Each session includes teaching, guided discussion, and weekly exercises to integrate the Practices into daily life.

Companion Guide

A detailed guide provides question prompts, session-by-session exercises, and space to write and reflect.

Recommended Resources

Additional recommended readings and podcasts offer a way to get the most out of the Practices.

Learn more by visiting practicingtheway.org/resources.

The Practicing the Way Course

An eight-session primer on spiritual formation

Two thousand years ago, Jesus said to his disciples, "Follow me." But what does it mean for us to follow Jesus today?

The Practicing the Way Course is an on-ramp to spiritual formation, exploring what it means to follow Jesus and laying the foundation for a life of apprenticeship to him.

WHAT'S INCLUDED

Eight Sessions

John Mark and other voices teaching on apprenticing under Jesus, spiritual formation, healing from sin, meeting God in pain, crafting a Rule of Life, living in community, and more

Exercises

Weekly practices and exercises to help integrate what you've learned into your everyday life

Guided Conversations

Prompts to reflect on your experience and process honestly in community

Companion Guide

A detailed workbook with exercises, space to write and reflect, and suggestions for supplemental resources

Learn more by visiting practicingtheway.org/resources.

Practicing the Way: *Be with him. Become like him. Do as he did.*

The first followers of Jesus developed a Rule of Life, or habits and practices based on the life of Jesus himself. As they learned to live like their teacher, they became people who made space for God to do his most transformative work in their lives.

Practicing the Way is a vision for the future, shaped by the wisdom of the past. It's an introduction to spiritual formation accessible to both beginners and lifelong followers of Jesus, and a companion to the Practicing the Way Course. This book offers theological substance, astute cultural insight, and practical wisdom for creating a Rule of Life in the modern age.

You can order your copy or get copies for your community at practicingtheway.org/book or through your preferred bookseller.

The Circle

Practicing the Way is a nonprofit that develops spiritual formation resources for churches and small groups learning how to become apprentices in the Way of Jesus.

We believe one of the greatest needs of our time is for people to discover how to become lifelong disciples of Jesus. To that end, we help people learn how to be with Jesus, become like him, and do as he did, through the practices and rhythms he and his earliest followers lived by.

All of our downloadable ministry resources are available at no cost, thanks to the generosity of The Circle and other givers from around the world who partner with us to see formation integrated into the Church at large.

To learn more or join us, visit practicingtheway.org/give.

For Facilitators

Before you begin, there are three easy things you need to do. (This should take only 10–15 minutes.)

01 Go to launch.practicingtheway.org, log in, create a group, and send a digital invitation to your community. This will give your group access to the Spiritual Health Reflection, videos, and all sorts of valuable extras. Encourage your group to bring along their Companion Guides to each session, as they contain the discussion questions and space to take notes.

- You can purchase a print or ebook version from your preferred retailer or find a free digital PDF version at launch.practicingtheway.org. We recommend the print version so you can stay away from your devices during the Practices, as well as take notes during each session. But we realize that digital works better for some.
- Note: You can order the Guides ahead of time and have them waiting when people arrive for Session 01, or encourage people to order or download their own and bring them to your gatherings.

02 Send a message to your group encouraging everyone to take the Spiritual Health Reflection before your first gathering, which can be found at launch.practicingtheway.org.

03 If your group has not been through the Practicing the Way Course, invite them to watch this short primer before you gather for Session 01 of this Practice.

For training, tips, and more resources for facilitating the Solitude Practice, log in to the Dashboard at launch.practicingtheway.org.

APPENDIX

Bonus Conversations

For those of you who want to spend longer sitting in this Practice, we've included an additional four weeks of material in this Guide to go deeper in Scripture and discussion.

You are welcome to pause in between sessions for these additional conversations or skip over them.

The Quiet Place

The Gospels reveal a recurring pattern of Jesus retreating and returning: retreating for solitude with his Heavenly Father and returning for loving service to others. This is the practice and purpose of solitude—that we would not be captured by the distractions of our noisy world or led by the many voices grasping for our attention, but that we would embrace the quiet with God, not only for the sake of our own souls but ultimately for the sake of others.

Read Mark 1v32–39

Discuss the Scripture

01 What stands out to you from today's passage?

02 How do you tend to respond to the needs and demands of others? What reflections do you have on Jesus' response of retreating for solitude and returning for service?

03 Jesus' time of retreat was filled with prayer. What kinds of activities typically fill your times of retreat? How does Jesus' example inspire or challenge you?

04 How could the goal of returning to serve others in love change how you structure and fill your times of retreat?

Discuss the practice

01 How did you decide to structure your time(s) of solitude this week?

02 Before engaging in this Practice, what kind of experience did you have with solitude? Would you say you felt more excited or hesitant going into this week's exercise? Why?

03 What kinds of distractions did you face during your time of solitude? How did you navigate these distractions emotionally and practically?

04 What expectations do you want to set for the next week to help you deepen your experience of solitude?

Repeat the exercise

For this week, we invite you to repeat the exercise on page 30 or to try the reach exercise if you have not already.

Encounter with Our Self

In the place of solitude, we are always confronted with ourselves—and often, through that encounter, we face our own pain, fears, and weariness. Like Elijah in the wilderness, this can overwhelm or exhaust us. Yet it is in this quiet place—whether in the stillness of a cave or the depths of our hearts—that we encounter not only ourselves but also the One who longs to tend to and speak to us. The question is: Will we endure long enough to know that he is as present in this solitary place as we are?

Read 1 Kings 19v1–12

Discuss the Scripture

01 What do you find most surprising about this story of Elijah's time in solitude?

02 What does Elijah encounter in himself in the wilderness (verses 01–05)? How does this align with or confront your own view of what takes place in solitude?

03 What reflections do you have on Elijah's honesty about his feelings and desires in prayer? How is this similar to or different from your own life of prayer?

04 If God sometimes speaks in a "gentle whisper," what do you think you can do in the short term to better arrange your life to hear from him?

Discuss the practice

01 What expectations did you have going into this week's time(s) of solitude, and how were they similar to or different from the previous week?

02 What was your experience like sitting with the feelings you identified? How did God meet you there?

03 What are your reflections on how easily our emotions can "backlog"? How did your time of solitude reveal this?

04 What did you notice happening in you as you gave God your feelings, your desires, and, ultimately, your trust?

Repeat the exercise

For this week, we invite you to repeat the exercise on page 50 or to try the reach exercise if you have not already.

Encounter with Our Enemy

In today's Psalm, we find the prayed words of a man who, according to Jewish tradition, is believed to have been hidden away in the wilderness. This prayer reveals who, not just what, we are to seek in the place of solitude. The Psalmist's words invite us to pursue solitude not just for our personal peace, but for a deeper encounter with the Person of God—so that in this place of subtraction, we become aware of the One who has been added to our lives and can never be taken away.

Read Psalm 63

Discuss the Scripture

01 What aspects of God's nature and character does the Psalmist highlight in this prayer from solitude? Which most stands out to you personally?

02 Consider the verbs in this Psalm, like *seek, beheld,* and *cling*. How do these verbs speak to what we are to do—or not do—in times of solitude?

03 Consider the feelings you have typically experienced in solitude. What part of this Psalm could you pray and return to in solitude to connect with God in those feelings?

04 The teaching from Session 03 and this Psalm describe the desert as a place of subtraction. What is one subtraction you can make to refine your times in solitude?

Discuss the practice

01 How was your experience practicing *Lectio Divina* this week? Which passage or passages of Scripture did you choose to slowly pray through?

02 What did God illuminate for you in his Word through this exercise?

03 After the teaching on the three enemies of the soul—the world, the flesh, and the devil—how did you notice those forces at work during your time of solitude?

04 What encouragement or prayer do you need from this community to continue facing the internal and external resistance in your times of solitude?

Repeat the exercise

For this week, we invite you to repeat the exercise on page 72 or to try the reach exercise if you have not already.

Encounter with Our God

By now, in your journey of practicing solitude, you are probably noticing (or are even overwhelmed by) the different voices that seem to grow louder as you grow quieter. That's normal—and it doesn't mean you're "doing" solitude wrong. It might actually mean you're doing it right. You're slowing down enough in silence to allow the noise of your internal world to surface. In this different kind of noise, the main task of every apprentice of Jesus becomes discernment—learning to recognize God's voice, the One who "calls" and "leads" us, amid all the others.

Read John 10v1–5

Discuss the Scripture

01 What was a time you recall listening to and following Jesus' voice in your life? In reflection, what did that experience teach you about discerning his voice?

02 What is significant for you personally about God's desire to "call" to you and "lead" you?

03 Reflecting on your time in this Practice, what have you identified as the "stranger's voice" that can emerge in solitude and that you do not want to follow?

04 What has God spoken to you about your identity and calling through the practice of solitude?

Discuss the practice

01 Describe your experience with listening prayer. What expectations did you have going into it, and how were they met or left unmet?

02 What other "voices" did you notice competing to drown out God's in this time? How did you navigate them?

03 What insecurities or fears do you have around discerning God's voice? How does discernment in community help you with those feelings?

04 What is one change you could make to your current life architecture to "de-noise" and better hear from God?

Repeat the exercise

For this week, we invite you to repeat the exercise on page 92 or to try the reach exercise if you have not already.

To inquire about ordering this Companion Guide in bulk quantities for your church, small group, or staff, contact churches@penguinrandomhouse.com.